Dear

Adventurist

brandi marie

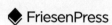 FriesenPress

Suite 300 - 990 Fort St
Victoria, BC, V8V 3K2
Canada

www.friesenpress.com

ISBN
978-1-5255-6192-4 (Hardcover)
978-1-5255-6193-1 (Paperback)
978-1-5255-6194-8 (eBook)

1. POETRY, SUBJECTS & THEMES, INSPIRATIONAL & RELIGIOUS

Distributed to the trade by The Ingram Book Company

Acknowledgements

I would like to thank my supportive loved ones who believe in anything I have my heart set on, and those who read this book and gave me the encouraging feedback I needed. We made it, thoughts to paper, paper to computer, and back to paper once again. I also need to thank myself. If not for my relentless intuition that has taken me on wild adventures, and my creativity that helps me transpose it all to art, this collection would be non-existent. Lastly, thank you to all who take the time now to read not only my words, but my heart and soul on printed pages.

Twitter: @13brandiii
Instagram: @brandi_was_here
Email: brandi.sawatzky13@gmail.com

This book is titled "Dear Adventurist," and it is just that; it is for someone out seeking more from this earth, for those who crave adventure and chase these dreams with every ounce of their hearts.

The first chapter is titled "You." Here, I write about things I feel I have learned along my own adventure and things I feel I have figured out. They're written to 'you' as advice or insight, or maybe they are simply a reminder that you aren't the only one to go through these obstacles on your journey.

Next, I write the chapter "I," these being all the things I feel I'm still learning along my journey and haven't fully understood yet. Maybe you, the reader, haven't either, and we can learn together. Or maybe you have and can recall a time before such growth and be able to recognize that growth in yourself as a positive.

"Them" is the chapter for people who don't feel an urge to explore, or who do but don't follow it through. Here, I aim to inspire their intuition or ignite some interest in them about the world that surrounds us, which is so easily forgotten or shut out. I invite them to join us on our adventure.

Lastly, I write "We," which is all about remembering how different we are but remembering that we are all different together. Everyone back home seems to have the same dreams and goals to go through together, so what, or who, do we have? Well, we have each other and this book. Just because our people may not be related or live nearby doesn't mean they aren't out there going through all the same challenges and emotions as we are. Adventurists need to remember there are so many of us, and we are living in our own guild and on our own terms, and that's perfectly acceptable. Because out in the world is where we find our happiness. And that's all anyone searches for in this life.

Personally, I've always felt like the only one with dreams to travel, because most everyone I knew wanted to go to school or straight into a trade. And when I was too afraid to go after what I wanted alone, it seemed logical to find happiness where everyone else did. But logic doesn't always work or win. Once I accepted myself with my differences and all, I realized how much happier I was, or more myself, and when I got out into the world I dreamed of, I met so many people living the same dreams.

I want to share all the doubts, emotions, stories, and adventures there are to be had in allowing yourself to follow your heart. So, if anyone ever feels as I did, maybe this could help them. Maybe my words could somehow give one adventurist a good place to start.

Dear Adventurist

Brandi Marie

Tanya ♡

thank you
for supporting
my dream

-B.

Dear Adventurist,

There is an undefined sense inside of you. It pulls at your curiosity and it dangles your soul's deepest desires ahead of you; always ahead of you. You forever feel a craving for more, for new, for everything and anything you have yet to know and experience.

The world, to you, is not a hidden door, but an open valley. There are times you see it from a distance, which satisfies your freedom; like from atop a great mountain. Other times, you find yourself right in on the action because you've made the decision to be there: to explore, to live.

You may not understand those who find contentment where they are and have always been. Those who don't know or don't care that the valley exists. Those who live off of dental plans, raises, and two weeks' vacation.

But you don't have to.

This life of yours is a story, and you're a conscious author. You are not a reader or a passenger. You drive life where you need to go to chase down who you are, because who you are is like lightning; ever changing and bold, spontaneous and reckless.

You are rare.

You are intimidating because of how dauntless you seem to others, but underneath it all, you are quite like anyone else, only you're on fire!

Your soul is forever burning; forever yearning for more.

And I know all of this because I, too, burn with these instincts and desires.

I'm an adventurist. Just like you.

Sincerely,

Unsigned, for our story has yet to begin.

Table of Contents

YOU

These are the things I've learned along my journey so far.
And maybe you have too.
And maybe you haven't gotten this far yet.
But I hope you do;
I hope this helps.

Dear Adventurist

I know you're scared.
Hell, I am too.
But I'm only scared for me,
And you're only scared for you.
This whole adventure thing takes guts.
But you're excited for me,
And I'm excited for you.
So why is it so easy to watch someone live their dreams,
Yet so hard to go after them ourselves?
Remember that
You are brave.
Hell, I am too.

It gets easier.
You cry less.
You gain comfort.
You lose stress.
But you'll always need your mom,
Her comforting words;
Her endless encouragement.

It gets easier.
Your mom will cry less.
She'll gain confidence in you.
Sometimes, she'll hold the stress for you,
But she's seen your bravery,
She knows you'll be fine.

The worst days
Make the best memories
While the best days
Make the worst worth it

What to expect when leaving home:

Tears,
or at the very least, a bit of a burn in the back of
your throat.

Unpreparedness,
an unsuspected summer snowfall when you didn't pack
a coat.

Laughter,
the uncontrollable kind reminding you to do more of it.

Deep Conversations,
getting to know someone so well in the smallest amount
of time.

Singing,
you're going to need something to do on that long
bus ride.

And Adventure,
but only if you're willing to throw yourself into it.

When you're ready to give up
Take a second to calm down
But if you're still feeling fed up
Turn around and head home

When you've had a rough day
Wash it off with your makeup
Remember that you get to call it
Whenever you've had enough

The scariest thing about growing up
is when you realize
you're considered a grown-up
and you're still scared.

But then you'll be on the bus, for hours
And you'll experience this sensation:

This uncontrollable,

Unstoppable,

Unavoidable,

Smile.

Part of it may be linked with claustrophobia
And restlessness,
A bit of deliria,
But it'll feel good.
It'll feel reassuring.
You are meant to be here.

Do your research
Reach out to that acquaintance who posted photos in the
same location
Which seems to keep calling out your name
Talk to them about their experience
Get your hopes up and hold your excitement in
Only long enough to exude that you're still sane

Then let it all out
But listen to your dad as he reminds you
when crossing the street to stop and look both ways
It's easy to get excited
And to lose yourself in the freedom
Just don't forget you still ought to stay safe

Something gets borrowed
And something gets broken
Something gets lost
Something else forgotten
Something goes wrong
And sometimes you cry
Some things are worth it
'Cause something will feel right

And if you're not ashamed of who you were, then you haven't lived.

Allow people to know you
And opportunities will fall
Like rain in the spring
Or leaves in the fall

When people know you
They'll think of your name
When opportunity rises
Like a morning's sun ray

If they give you the chance
Just be as you are
You'll soar through any sky
Like a bold shooting star

Find someone who looks like you:
Lost, scared, a little confused.
Ask them if they'd like to join in
On whatever it is that seems foreign.
Cities are usually where you start out
But they're intimidating and difficult to go about.
So sit down where there's Wi-Fi and people
And make one friend who's just as scared as you.

You will get homesick
And you will call Mom
She'll tell you things
Like you're brave and you're loved
You'll pretend that you're stronger than even she thinks
you are
Then you'll hang up the phone and cry even harder
than before
But the tears will run dry
And the time will go by
You'll fall in love with this adventure
And the uncertainty
is far from what you'll remember

Don't be blind
Don't close your mind
Open your eyes
And you will find
That people are people
And people are kind

Dear Adventurist

Who are you?
Who are you with?
What are your plans?
What's on the agenda?
Where are you from?
Where are you headed?
When did you get here?
When will you return?
Why are you here?
Why did you choose this?

Just a glimpse at the conversations you will grow sick of,
But hold them anyways, and always, always listen.
The questions may be all the same,
But the answers will continue to change.
And not just theirs, but yours.
Their answers may inspire you to venture off course.

People come and people go
They teach you things so that you know
How to live and how to grow
And when it's time to let love go

A Soulmate

love fills our hearts
love fills our minds
but only we
can fill our time

love will come
and love will go
so spend time searching
within your soul

your soul is made of waves and fire
create the bridge of life you desire
search your soul both far and wide
for love will find you, every time

when you're at peace,
your thoughts and heart
will settle in
and play their part

love can breed
off hearts and minds
but it's called a soulmate
so waste no time

When you lose someone special
You set sail to discover yourself
If you're incapable of manning this ship
You find someone else

Then sometimes you grow good
At this discovery of yourself
But you grow lonely and lose who you are
Whilst finding someone else

He offers his hand to the girl lost at sea
She anchors and takes it oh so willingly
Two boats rock together at the waves of the bay
No longer must she learn how to find her own way

An alliance takes form for survival
A reliance takes form for revival

But that's not love

Love is a desire
A passion
A fire
Love is understanding
A bond
A respecting of another being

There are no needs
Nor uses
Nor abuses
In love
There are no expectations
Nor short-ended
One-sided conversations
Not in love

Love is not two boats
Love is not two anchors

Love is two independent sailors
Taking on the sea together
Seeing all life can be
Forever

Wouldn't you rather be lonely alone,
Than lonely while you're with someone?

Your heart's in your left.
Your head's in your right.
Too bad you aren't left-handed,
To dominate this fight.

The battle between
How you think
And how you feel,
Is difficult to outweigh
What is logical
From what is real.

With your dominant hand,
You're only fooling yourself.
To hold your head in your right,
Confuses comfort with doubt.

So put your thoughts to rest.
And rest your right hand on your chest.
It will tell you why it beats,
You simply must relax,
And believe.

you are never in control of how you feel.
just familiar.
and when you feel you've lost control over what you
are experiencing,
remind yourself:

you never have control over these things.

we gain a sense of comfort in certain ways we tend to feel.
but just because a new feeling is unfamiliar,
doesn't mean you've lost control.

you can't lose anything you've never possessed.

Let the difficult things inspire you
Take that sadness and ask yourself why you feel this
Take your anxiety and learn what disrupts it
Get mad and then figure out how to induce calmness
Get even without hurting people's feelings
Let the difficult things happen
Let them inspire you
Let the worst make you better
Help yourself to grow

Plant yourself where the opportunity for growth is limitless.

You are a flower
You wilt when it's rainy
In some places you even get crushed
You're so dainty

You are a flower
You tear petals off for love
From those who claim
You're never quite enough

You are a flower
You need water, soil, and light
And a little bit of acceptance
To make yourself shine bright

You are a flower
So, why have you planted roots in concrete?
Allow yourself to find
A better place to feel complete

It doesn't really matter where you go when your soul is telling you to leave. It could be an hour outside of town or halfway across the globe.

Just go!

Go because something in you is telling you to go; is willing you to go.

Sometimes, our bodies know better than we do as to what they need or where they need to be. I believe when we're ready to grow, sometimes there isn't enough room to do so where we are.

That's when our hearts tell us we crave change, because we, ourselves, are changing. And it's easier to change when our surroundings do.

Leave your comfort zone to try something different and wild!

Leave home to find somewhere new for a while!

It's not only going to be fun. And it's not only going to be hard. But when you're done, you'll gain a new perspective on where you've been and who you are.

I know you're scared, but it was your idea in the first place.

So, go because you aren't ready.

And somewhere along the way, I guarantee you'll find out that you are.

Allow them in
Even if and when
They hurt you.

And then allow them in again
Because chances are meant to be given
When they're taken.

Perhaps there are noises we despise hearing:
Nails on a chalkboard,
Creaks in the night,
But when the voice in your head is speaking,
Listen.
That is you.
And that is the you who knows better than you do.
Not all things that are hard to hear,
Are meant to be blocked out.

You may not be able to give a scientific reason
or a thought-out justification
as to why you are where you are
But you don't need one

If you are happier where you are than where you were
You did something right
And you don't need to be able to answer the questions
begging you why

Your motive isn't what they tell you,
it's not where you started out.

Your purpose lies beneath the surface,
they'll never get what that's about.

So follow what you have inside,
forget about those flashing signs.

Who knows, you may end up surprised,
that you can make your stars align.

Follow your heart
And run from your mother
She loves you too much
to not act as your cover
She'll shield you from rain
she'll block you from fire
But if inside you it burns
you must rise with desire
Kiss her goodbye
then leave her behind
She can't do this for you
She'll understand why

There will be days you don't explore
Maybe you're too tired
Maybe you're just bored
There will be days you wish you were home
Maybe you miss it
Maybe you miss someone
But when you feel you've done everything you came here
to do
Think of the rest as a bonus round
with extra time to explore you

It's a steady pace.
It's a shoe untied.
To catch your breath;
to count each step you take.
It's a moonlit night.
It's an early morning hike.
To catch the sunrise;
to start the day off right.
It's the sun in your eyes.
It's the coffee awakening your soul.
To a new opportunity;
to another day,
in
    your
        life.

Simply by being out there,
you're a lot closer to the answers you don't know you're
looking for,
than you are being close to any singular other being.

Trust your instincts
Challenge yourself
Push the limits
Bandage yourself
Trust your heart
Treat yourself
Bend until you break
Mend yourself
You are indestructible
Remember that about yourself
You will adapt and bounce back
Believe in yourself

Suck it up.

Stop crying.

And I don't mean to tell you to pull yourself together,

but pull yourself together.

Take a breath.

Take a minute.

Remember one thing you love

and then get lost in it.

Sing a song.

Dance a little.

Call up your dad and laugh a little.

No one knows you better than you do,

So, figure out how to relax,

and keep doing you.

You may lose sight of who you thought you were
while you're busy gaining new perspective.
But never feel any less than assured
that you're figuring out what your heart is.
Your heart is not this constant thing.
It changes course as the weather.
Follow it through autumn, summer, spring,
and come winter, you'll understand yourself better.

It's right before you fall asleep and right before you fully wake up. It's after yoga class when you lay on the ground in savasana. It's when you're lost in the movement of walking and you forget where you're going. It's in that one song that you sing as loud as you can whilst driving down an endless road. It's every second you spend physically close to the one person you feel most emotionally close to. This sensation of losing yourself and losing grasp of your substance is when you know you're at peace. Being so far away from reality and so far away from yourself substantially is when you are most one with yourself. When you are most you. In each moment that you care less about yourself and what others think, you gain perspective on who you are. And it should always be that way.

So do more things for you. Turn off your phone and fall asleep peacefully. Work really hard and then take a moment to appreciate what you just did, whether working or working out. Walk for miles following your thoughts, not a map. Sing louder than you vocally should. Embrace the time you spend with whoever it is that you feel most comfortable with in every way possible.
Because that's who you are, and that's what you love.
So be who you love.

I

These are things I'm still trying to figure out.
Writing about them always helps me to understand what
goes on in my thoughts.
These are for me.
Although I'm willing to give them to you too.

I am a story teller.
But they say, "Write what you know."
So, I had to live a life full
Of tearing myself apart
And building myself back up,
Until it was enough
To give to you.
Until I could live to tell the stories that would satisfy and fulfill
Young hearts and minds
Very much like mine.

It is my story you read.
It is yours that's read.

She appreciated the things in her life;
they were enough for her.
But her soul screamed to reach for more,
So she left "enough" behind her.

I was seventeen
And stress seemed
To rule me.
I let things build up in my mind 'til I screamed.
I never saw the full picture, I only saw screens.
I used to allow those things to ruin me.

I'm twenty-one.
I don't let things stress me out.
There were so many things I seemed worried about,
Yet all of those things turned out
To only be doubts.
Turns out,
I've still got none of those things figured out.

I'm nearly twenty-two
And something in me has changed.
I no longer care how much time that I take.
The tigers used to roar and escape
From their cages.
But I've learned to let them roam,
And I taught them to be tame.

the moon waxes and wanes
the waves push and pull
my heart heightens and tames
my soul comes and goes

There are days where I don't want to get out of bed
There are days where the beer seems to have slept in my head
There are days where the coffee does nothing to help
There are days where I feel there's no more to be felt

There are times where I list things I wish to be doing
There are times where instead I do nothing at all
There are times where work is my main reason for moving
There are times where I feel if I stand I could fall

There are days where I don't speak to anyone
There are days where I seem not to have any fun
There are days where I'm right where I've begun
There are days I wish I would grow and become

There are nights where anxiety resides in my brain
There are nights where asleep seems a long ways away
There are nights where my nightmares resemble my days
There are nights where I fear all my fears never fade

There are days where I doubt everything that I'm doing
There are times where I feel I should be more than I can
There are nights where I refuse to admit that I'm proving
I am exactly who I need to be right where I am

They say you learn and grow and change so much after
something like this.

I never believed them.
I believed it would be fun, and maybe at times frightening.
I believed it would show me brand new sights and all
new highs.
I believed I would come home with stories but still fold
right back in to where I left off.
I was wrong.

I learned so many things that would forever broaden
my perspective.
I outgrew any mould I had been stuck in, having to re-
establish where I fit in.
And I changed.
I took my old self to all new places, physically
and mentally,
Then I left her behind,
lost somewhere along the way.
And that was okay.

Because I had a stronger, braver, bolder version of myself
to bring all the way back home.

And she lives my life better than I ever could
before I met her.

They were right.

My curiosity is only as large as this world is.
It's rather unlikely I'll venture further than the earth's
eight corners.

I guess in a way, you have it worse.
Because you have to live with the ghost of me,
All over your hometown.

But maybe I have it worse.
Because I have to live with missing you,
And your hometown.

The greatest fear I have is wasting my youth,
Which outweighs any fear I have about living it.

Sure, I guess I'm scared.
But I believe it's only because the people I love are scared for me.

I'm scared for change, but above that, I'm scared of remaining the same. I don't want to fade into the old patterns and routines that I'm running from in the first place.

I'm not as scared to go as I am to come back home. Because what if the people I'm leaving behind won't be here for me when I'm back in due time?

I'm scared of growing on this new adventure and outgrowing the life I'll have to return to. But I'm more scared to stop growing into all my potential.
I guess I am scared.

"I'll be happy when the sun starts shining,"
I tell myself, gloomy day after gloomy day.
They drag on just the same.

And it's finally here, but I'm beginning to fear,
that I'm only happy because I'm leaving.

I'm only smiling to be freeing myself from whatever seems
to be holding me down.

In this town, I've found a home.
But my wings can't stand another tie;
another hole.

Now I must fly,
I must find out how to be whole.
It may lead me astray,

Or, it may guide me back home.

I often find myself sitting on the ocean floor.

As to the reason I have drowned, I'm unsure.

But I do know I can't hold my breath for too long.

And even with no energy to swim,

I'll float back up again,

And again.

What's the point?
Why do we fight?
Give me the answers.
What is life?

Close my eyes.
Deep breath in.
Dry my face.
Believe again.

Laugh with friends.
Drink a beer.
Sing, or run.
I'm happy here.

It's funny because you're here.
And I'm here.

You're a few streets away.
And I can't find a single word to say.

And I'm looking forward to being there.
While you're still here.

Because I think being five hundred miles away.
Will give us both more words to say.

It's not the leaving that scares me,
it's what I'd be leaving behind.

I'm an adventurous soul
who exercises her wild side
I'm moving five hundred miles from home
while my mother just sighs
She knows as well as anyone in my life
that I can't be tied down
nor can I be held too tight
So when I say I'm going away
again
She knows better than to ask me to stay

I've yet to figure out
whether it's my heart or my soul
But something inside of me
tells me when and where to go
This feeling soars me above
It also buries me in lows
But life is better experienced in waves
than it is to coast

So fly me like an airplane
and drown me like a shipwreck
I'd like to touch the moon
and whatever else my heart plans next

brandi marie

I take the path that forever bends
And see it through until it ends
I won't stop for thirst or drought
I have to know what life's about
Follow me only if you dare
For if you can't keep up
I can't seem to care
My life is guided by my intuition
Any other voice I choose not to listen
So take my hand or let me go
There are far too many things I simply wish to know

I was given four walls
to call my own.
I was given four walls
to feel at home.

I've painted these walls many times in my life.
I've hung art,
I've pinned maps,
I've placed tiny strings of lights.

But these walls, they hold secrets,
they hold keepsakes,
all my dreams.

If it weren't for these walls,
I wouldn't dream a damn thing.
And if I never left them behind,
these walls would contain only broken things.

I was given four walls
to call my own.
I was given four walls
to come back home.

I see the world in black and white
and **bold**.
And you see things in a shade of grey
that I wish I could turn to gold.
If only you would let me hold you.
It could be us against the world,
no matter the hue.

I tiptoe around myself in a sprint.
It distracts my unstable mind I've felt stuck in.
A means of steering clear of the mental state I wish not to
be in.
I tiptoe around myself in a sprint.

I tiptoe around myself in a sprint.
I run to places I've never been.
I run from the faces I refuse to let in.
I tiptoe around myself in a sprint.

I tiptoe around myself in a sprint.
I don't do this on purpose,
I do this because I can.
When I don't feel happy,
I distract myself until I am.

I've gotten so used to this free-spirited mind,
It's no longer a necessity in order to enjoy living my life.
I no longer tiptoe around,
I allow myself to sprint.

Do you miss home?

Feeling at home is a state of mind.
And mine's at peace out here.
I cannot miss a place that exists within myself.

Out of sight
       and out of mind
I'm starting to see
       you weren't ever mine
But when your name
       lights up my phone
I silently wish
       I could call you my home

Out of sight
       and out of mind
When you're away
       I'm truly fine
I live as if
       you don't exist
Until you do
       and my heart   skips

Out of sight
       and out of mind
You're not here
       for me to find
But if you were
       you know I would
When I think of you
       I believe love is good

I've learned many things today
which I lay down
and give myself credit for
before I drift away

But when I awake
I'm given an entire new day
to learn even more things
To be grateful for
before I drift away

Is my time sacrificed
Will I regret spending it all on myself
Do I fear loneliness
Or is this all going to be worth it

Is my time well spent
Will I bleed to self-benefit
Do I embrace this loneliness
To make my adventure worth it

I'm more fearful my time will be wasted
Not working toward discovering myself
I would take all the loneliness in this world
If it meant making my life worth it

I still get nervous.
I worry about what I'll eat,
If they'll have coffee for me in the morning times.
I worry about getting sick on the plane,
And whether or not the sun will shine.

But then I have to go through security and act courageous.
And the act alone is enough to remind me that
I am courageous.
I can do this.

When I focus on something bigger than me
In small detail
I forget about the small things
That seem too big to get around

I like that I don't know anyone.
And I like that I don't have to.
I'm easy to get to know,
But difficult to get through to.

I like how you aren't here.
And I love how I don't miss you.
I've been so busy getting to know myself,
I didn't even notice I was getting over you.

I didn't mean to get your hopes up.
And I never meant to forget you.
But everything I've learned about myself,
I've learned to love, without you.

I didn't ask to fall this hard
this fast
But it was a mountain I had already fallen down
And in the science of falling
I was up
I've been to the top and experienced the journey
So of course
Of course I would do it time and time again
for even another second of the view atop our mountain

I learned about distance,
and about love.
I learned about the land,
I gained perspective from up above.
I also gained self-respect,
and I acquired this because
I learned that certain people aren't
all we make up and judge.
I'm not as good at judging character
as I always thought I was,
but I learned that discovering myself through adventure
is more than enough.
I've enjoyed my experience here,
knowing I've only just begun
to scratch the surface of understanding
and testing exactly what it is
I'm made up of.

brandi marie

Out of all the places in the world,
nothing feels like coming home.

The boy I saw over the summer
was like going to Mexico: hot,
drunk, well-deserved. Yet not
somewhere you can stay for
longer than ten days.

                    —loneliness

And the boy I fell for the other
year was like New Zealand:
Beautiful. Similar to home, yet
far from it, in distance and in
reality.

                    —in another life

The one I kissed right after you
felt like Italy: refreshing,
rejuvenating and as foreign as
the tongue they speak.

                    —too soon

Then there was the boy I met
in school like New York:
overwhelming with new
opportunities, but just another
city. Full of lost hopes and
broken dreams.

—too much

And there's more; more faces
that remind me of all the places
I've been or would like to go. But
none that leave me feeling the
way I do when I get back home.

—you

Out of all the faces in the world,
no one else quite feels like home.

You were such a beautifully full-grown pine tree
You stood tall and proud in a forest amongst those
beneath you
like me
I was a young spruce, hiding in your shadow
But that's no place to try and allow myself to grow
There isn't any room for potential beneath your
thick branches
There isn't any room for discovery in these circumstances
I'm apologetic that I had to leave your side
You've since grown cold without me to confide in
But I believe my actions were justified
The minute I outgrew your shadow
And came alive

I'm impulsive.
I'm uncontrollable.
I make mistakes and hurt people,
Although all of it is unintentional.

I'm an emotional mess.
I'm a hopeless romantic.
I don't own a filter.
But I think a lot,
only, after I've acted.

I push the boundaries.
I mess up a lot.
I don't know what to do with it all,
Yet I'm still full of love.

I'm a perfectionist.
I obsess over stupid things.
I cry over spilled milk,
And work myself up over nothing.

If I've made up my mind,
There's no going back.
I'm relentless in taking what I want from life,
Knowing one day life will take it all back.

I'm human.
I've heard all the lessons.
But unless it's firsthand,
I refuse to learn them.

THEM

These are for them.
Those who keep their bucket list in the back of
their closet.
Those whose lives could flash before them tomorrow and
they would have nothing to show for it.
Those who choose to settle.
Those who choose to sleep.
Those who live their lives stuck on repeat.

I wish to inspire you.
But your wish must be to be inspired.

There is nothing wrong with them.
In fact, there's more of them:
People who are content
with what life has given them.

Climb a Mountain with Me

and then you will see
the beauty in our land
from a vantage point
where things become
much simpler to understand

Climb a Mountain with Me

and test who you are
there are things you're capable of
that will strengthen your heart

Climb a Mountain with Me

and set yourself free
of an image the media
suggests you should be

Climb a Mountain with Me

and overanalyze your thoughts
until you open your eyes
and realize you're lost

Climb a Mountain with Me

but don't try to keep up
there are things to be learned
from yourself up above

don't tell me that you're jealous
of all my evidence
that I've been present
in my own life

when you hold no intention
to go after anything
that you wish you had
in your own life

If you're happy
with your two weeks' vacation

if you're content
with your backyard and your fence

If you've settled
for never seeing past your city's limits

Then forget it

My job isn't to change your mind
My job is to explore mine
But if you aren't going to explore yours
There's no one who will do it for you

How do you measure success?
Is it about the grades you received in high school?
Or the post-secondary education your student loan
bought you?
Is it the job that drains your energy?
Or the mortgage that drains your bank account?
Is it the car that takes you nowhere?
Is that what success is all about?

I measure my success in stories.
Lessons I've learnt from all my exploring.
I measure my success in happiness.
The smile that says I've been doing my best.
I measure my success in others.
Those who stand by me and those I inspire.

Allow me to inspire you.
Do one thing you wouldn't normally do.
Go someplace that may surprise you.
Go out to see the world,
and the world may show you, you.

There are people who travel to post something picturesque.
There are people who travel because someone else paid for it.
There are people who travel for jobs or education.
There are people who travel with too many expectations.
There are people who travel without any intentions.
There are people who travel to get away from their problems.
But these people who travel are not adventurists.
These people are just people who pretend to know what
adventure is.

Maybe
You like to hold your academic accomplishments and
health benefits over me
But if I ever meet your grandbabies
They'll never quit raving
About all my stories
And the best part will be
When they ask you why you don't have any

Stop buying things to pass the time
End the cycle of barely getting by
Invest in being more than just fine
Change the way you live your life

It's not always about the places,

But rather the experiences.

And I can't stand here and make promises

That any of it will be flawless.

But they know that.

Probably better than I do,

Probably better than any of us do.

They know that with every blessing comes a curse,

And for every better follows a worse.

They're smart.

But to me,

A life isn't lived if it's stuck in that part.

To ride a wave,

Or walk along sand.

To sit in place,

Or to take that chance.

I know you're happy
Living vicariously through me
But the pictures you see
Are nothing
Compared to reality

A lonely field under lingering fog
Minds are closed and hearts are locked
Time stands still yet humans walk
Love is real but passion has stopped

A city sky over starless eyes
The air is clean yet the truth still hides
Honesty bleeds beneath bandaged lies
Answers are clear but the questions still why

It's
easier
to
fear
something
you're
used
to
being
scared
of
than
to
imagine
the
degree
of
fear
you're
facing
with
the
unknown.

They call me brave.
Wide-eyed, and in disbelief
that a girl such as me
could be capable of wild things.
Aren't you scared? they say.
Full of fears themselves;
fears which I do not possess.
How could I be scared of a world that I already live in?
They're scared because it's the same world,
Only they're just existing.

When you limit yourself, you're building fences in
your mind.
I've worked way too hard at knocking down all of mine.
Your thoughts are in line, yet full with literalness.
While my thoughts are chasing an imagination,
Who is limitless.

They don't have the money.
They don't have the time.
They don't have the courage
Or the bravery like mine.

They don't care to go.
They don't care to see
A world that's full of people
They admire such as me.

But what have they gained
From missing out on their lives?
How to make up excuses,
Until the day that they die?

How to get stuck in routine,
How to lie, how to hide
From a world worth exploring.
Will you get out there?
Or just get by.

I'm not brave enough
Or crazy
I'm not that fit
Or thin enough
I'm not organized
I don't have the time

But the truth is
You're just not willing enough

Everyone is enough
I am
He is
She is
They are
We are

There must be something that makes you want to get out
of bed
Something that you've been looking forward to forever
Some idea you can't get out of your head
Something you can't wait until we can do together

Isn't that enough
Isn't just that
An adventure

Maybe they know better than we do
About borders
Lines
Comfort zones
Safety bubbles
Maybe they have a better picture in their minds
About what's really out there in the world
But how can they know anything
About something they've never even seen

Adventure has no wings.
She has no magic wand or fairy dust.
Her teeth aren't pristinely white,
Nor is she a stranger to a world of lust.
She cannot see the future,
and she knows not of your past.
But if you believe within her,
She can make that feeling last.

I think I get it
Home is a place of comfort
a space of freedom and routine
all at once

I think I get it
Relationships require effort
a desire for presence
in order to succeed

I think I get it
Careers provide fulfillment
a purpose for living
out of all that time spent working

I think I get it

But then I get out there
Where perception is what you make it
Where your soul becomes awakened
And there's no way
I could fake this

I don't think I get it
But I do get this

I don't mean to imply
There's a damned thing wrong with their lives
I'm just happy with mine
And wish to explain or show why

This travelling thing is hard.
It takes money,
It takes guts.
Two things none of us have got.
But if you fake it 'til you make it,
and save up one more paycheque,
All this travelling thing takes,
is heart.

Adventure doesn't exist in different countries.
It doesn't greet you the second you step off that airplane,
As there's no guarantee it'll accompany you on that train.
It won't just join you at dinner for a meal and a drink,
Or wash up from the tide, if that's what you think.

You don't need to go anywhere to find adventure.
There is no secret to its location.
It's something that lives inside us all.
There's no complicated equation.

Just step into your backyard,
or walk around the block.
Head over to your neighbour's house,
With no intentions but to talk.
Ride a bike down the street,
then climb a mountain down the road.
Swim in lakes or ocean waves,
or simply walk along the coast.

An adventure is seeking not for a place,
but somewhere we can feel whole.
It's escaping that dreadful everyday pace,
and breathing life back into our souls.

WE

We all feel different.
And we all feel alone.
But there's so many of us out there.

We all get so caught up in our adventure,
We forget we need company;
We forget to give company.

So, if you are like me,
I hope this gives you comfort at times when you feel alone
on your adventure.

This isn't just my story
And it isn't just yours
This is our story
And the us I'm talking about is bigger than you and I
There are so many of us who share this journey
And if you're one of us
I wish to share my journey with you

We're stronger than the delicate
flower who loses petals season
after season. We're the soil and
the sun, which the flower continues
to grow from year after year.

y.

a

w

There are times in life we need to fly a

b i r d s

Some of us do this as　　　　, others as　　　　.

b a l l o o n s

They are more selfless,
but we're allowed to be selfish now and again.

They are more established,
but our free spirits take us places they've never been.

They are more honest,
but we only lie to ourselves when we try to be like them.

Everybody has something:
Whether it's motion sickness,
Homesickness, seasickness,
Or plain old anxiety.
But we encounter other travellers
And we don't recognize they're strugglers.
No one has a perfect trip.
No one has a seamless trek.
Remember we're never completely on our own.
Every adventurist has experienced things we do not know.

Share your stories.
You'll feel good about surviving the worst,
And you'll feel better when you share with someone else
Who laughs at having survived worse.

An adventure consists of mountains,
or fires,
waves of an ocean,
backroads and tires.
It could be upon streets in the city,
or under starry night skies,
a walk through the park,
or a long summer's drive.
Boating,
or diving,
climbing,
zip-lining.
Cheers-ing,
or floating,
music festival going.
It's next to the mashed potatoes at your family dinner,
or in the popcorn during movie nights with your sister.
An adventure comes in many shapes and sizes.
But the people you share it with,
are the ultimate prizes.

Experience is so very vital to our existence
Persist to acquire all that is offered
Embrace this

We are wildly misunderstood.
And not only by others who simply do not live the same
lifestyle as us,
But by ourselves.
We are not out chasing new locations and faces only,
We are out to chase ourselves,
Our souls.
And allowing ourselves to do so,
Allows us to work toward who we are.
And we may never fully understand every depth and
corner of who we are.
But at least by following our hearts,
We know we are on the right journey.

You never know if you're dirty or tanned.
The one thing you can count on
is a change in plans.

Suddenly, it's luxury to find a bar of soap.
Your expectations shrink but you grow in hope.
You wear yourself out almost as much as your clothes.

And replace your limited backpack space with a whole new
wardrobe to bring home,
Along with stories and photos and recipes to try out.

But the one thing you can bring with you, yet cannot
share around,
Is this wonderful,
mind opening,
perspective altering,
Humbling,
difficult and rewarding,
challenging and forthcoming,
E x p e r i e n c e

Make plans. Take breaks.
Take naps. Make a mistake.
Skip ahead. Fall behind.
Fall in bed with a random guy.
Dive in. Climb out.
Drive away from all the doubt.
Jump up. Lay down.
Lie in silence. Or be the sound.

Sometimes we get so wrapped up in our routine lives,
We don't realize
How much baggage we're truly carrying around.
Sometimes all it takes
Is a simple drive
To clear our minds.

Life is about making choices.
And I'm going to tell you there are no wrong ones to
be made.
Choose to make a choice.
And make it because it feels right.
And if you find out you were wrong after all,
At least you tried.
Life is about learning from our mistakes.
Choose to make them.

We're supposed to be scared.
We're supposed to be wild.
We're young only once,
Let's set the world on fire.

We're supposed to be brave.
We're supposed to be tame.
We're not breaking the rules,
If we made up the game.

We crave a feeling more than anything. It's never truly about the destination, or the activities, the souvenirs, or the memories. We experience this fulfilling sensation that our inner compasses have guided us in the right direction. To be exactly where we are for this moment. This moment of pure bliss. A place where mind, body, and soul have come together to release any tension and to simply be. And to simply feel. That's why we travel.

And that's also why we go home. We crave a feeling. And home provides such a peaceful one, especially after travelling induces such a wild one.

when things are falling to pieces
and everything is wrong
think of all the people
waiting to laugh along

Tears don't run like rivers
Tears don't rise like waves
Emotions run like gravity
Emotions rise without shame

We feel a certain obligation to get out there.

To do everything we can,

and see anything we can.

As if our duty in life is to experience it all.

For ourselves,

and for those whose commitments lie within borders;

within boundaries.

We take it upon ourselves to oblige to the mission of travel.

For there are those who feel devoted to a life without such.

We mustn't take this life for granted.

For thousands, or millions, of people don't have the options
as we do

to go anywhere and do anything this world offers us.

Hard work can earn this in our lives,

but there are many who work hard to simply get by.

And the truth is: we are privileged.

It is our obligation to take full advantage of the opportunities
we can choose from.

And it is our duty to rise to the full bravery we have
been given.

Travelling can be like choosing a surprise bag.
We're excited about whatever could be inside;
Sometimes it's all highs,
Others come with lows.
But no matter the surprise,
It doesn't stop us from trying.

Everyone is born into a life.

Maybe everyone gets reborn into a new one.

Ours is more than just to survive.

It's our turn to explore and have fun.

And as simple as it may sound,

Not everyone has the means or courage to fulfill this.

Life gave us the legacy.

Life chose us to be bound,

To a world fruitful of experience.

And a world within ourselves we hold success.

We take risks, chances, and hands.
We farewell our comfortability,
And invite our independence.
We milk opportunity,
We drink coffee when we can.
We eat whatever we're given,
And make, then ditch, our plans.
But we do it because we're driven,
And we do it because we can.

Accept the offer like a mother's hand whilst crossing
the street.
Back then, she kept us safe from the world.
Now the world offers to keep us safe from ourselves.

People who haven't travelled don't know what weighs the opposite side of the scale. They don't know that there are things that outweigh the risks involved. There are things so enriching in the world that they've never experienced. And because we take those risks and believe our lives will benefit from any new experiences, they do; we do. We are the opposite side of that scale. We are the risk. We are enriched.

We are all in search of our purpose
The longer the search
The more we grow nervous
We are all in search of our person
The further we search
The more we grow nervous

But we're all searching
And we're all growing
It's less about discovering
And more about journeying

Finding happiness is a central goal in our lives
But it's also okay to lose it sometimes
A mood is not meant to be a permanent condition
Finding a good balance is the real mission

"Live less out of habit and more out of intent."

Going about each day in routine steps and just sticking to whatever is normal isn't really living. It's almost the exact opposite; as if you're dead, just a zombie following a set path and never venturing from that.

But to live with intent is what I would classify as really living. Here, one sets goals and reaches them. Here, there is a purpose to our actions as opposed to blandly going through the motions. And it may not mean changing what we do, but how we do it.

For instance, every morning I brush my teeth. Now, I don't speak for everyone here, but I like to make a habit out of brushing my teeth. So, of course, there are those days. Maybe I have to be up too early, or I'm just hungover or exhausted or lazy, and I just brush my teeth without second thought. But we all have those other days too. Like when you jump out of bed and are excited for your day, whether it's Christmas morning or time to go snowboarding. But on these days, I nearly forget to brush my teeth, or I try to get it done so fast that I spill toothpaste on my shirt and have to change.

What I am getting at is not that brushing your teeth faster will keep the dentist away, but that when you actually think about the motions you go through, they become more of a human action than that of a zombie. And to live on this Earth, I think it's best to live as who we are, human. Which is to rush with excitement and to make mistakes that cost us time or regret, and to really live with intention. We have a purpose here; the least we can do is try to fulfill that.

I believe we're always growing,
Which is why we think we lose sight of who we are.
But really,
We just outgrew who we were.

There are no requirements nor measurements;
no recipes, or secret ingredients.
An adventurist meets no standard,
and counts stars over followers on Instagram.
We have dreams that can't sleep,
and goals within reach.
We have stories to write,
and the whole world to see.

So, if there's a voice in your head you can never turn off,
And the desire to explore like an itch or a cough,
When you become restless in places you've seen too
much of,
And you're happy with it all, yet it's never enough:

You can call yourself an adventurist.
Say it in your head, and then whisper it out loud.
Tell it to one friend, and then scream it to a crowd.
However you wear it, put it on like a crown.
I am an adventurist,
and I am damn proud.

About the Author

Debut author Brandi Marie is a seasoned world traveller who has visited New Zealand, Australia, Cambodia, Laos, and Thailand, among others. While on her travels, she wrote her poems and reread them to help her find the strength within herself and the bravery she needed to continue on. She also learned her limits and, when the time came, she returned home. She now lives with her parents and sister in Aldergrove, BC, where she plans her next chapter of adventures.

A Note from the Author

Thank you for taking this adventure with me. Reading a book can sometimes take you to places you've never been. But in this case, I hope my words can take you somewhere new in actuality or help you through an unfamiliar journey you're already on. Regardless of where you are, I appreciate you being here with me right now. The writing and production behind getting these pages into your hands has been a new and exciting one for me, and I'm looking forward to hearing what kind of adventures this book has brought to you.

Brandi Marie

Twitter: @13brandiii
Instagram: @brandi_was_here
Email: brandi.sawatzky13@gmail.com